I Leave You Quarters
love from beyond the clouds

Dr. Cheryl Robinson

All rights reserved. This book or any portion thereof may not be reproduced or used in any manner whatsoever without the express written permission of the publisher except for the use of brief quotations in a book review.

Story Copyright © 2023 by Dr. Cheryl Robinson

Printed in the United States of America

Illustrations are used under the permitted licensing agreement from Canva pro membership 2023.

Thank you to the amazing photographers for sharing your creativity:

Getty Images: Cover: @markdanielwilson, Page 7: @harrymason, Page 10: @naranyu, Page 11: @enduro, Page 12: @canbedone, Page 13: @leembe, Page 14: @julia, Page 16: @hannator, Page 19: @nadianb, Page 20: @scopioimages, Page 23: @solarseven, Page 25: @bk_kang, Page 26: @nito100, Page 27: @gafvision, Page 31: @usamedeniz, Page 32: @mg_54, Page 34: @anyaberkut, Page 37: @natashababenko, Page 40: @brayavuz, Page 42: @aldomurillo, Page 43: @andreka. — — Canva: Page 15: @julieayers, Page 28: @dreamartist, Page 35: @pixelshot Getty Images Signature: Page 17, @gbrundin, Page 22: @jecapix, Page 29/36: @peopleimages, Page 33: @in-future — — Getty Images Pro: Page 38: @choochart choochaikupt —— Pixaby: Page 8: @avi_acl, Page 9: @pexels—2286921, Page. 18: @piro4d, Page 21: @hans, Page 24: @Jack ou-dl, Page 30: @sharky, Page 39: @BAEhdQmC5rk, Page 41: @jakob-wiesinger

Creative Renegade Media
New Jersey

ISBN: 978-0-9856849-9-0

creativerenegademedia.com

The Back Story

Ever since my grandfather passed away, I find dimes in the most random places. I learned about the spiritual theory that loved ones who have passed away, leave coins behind to let people know they're thinking of them and still love them.

My friend's mother recently crossed over, and during one of our conversations I shared my stories of finding dimes. Soon after, he started finding quarters in the most unusual places.

As his milestone birthday approached, I had a dream with him and his mother. We sang *Happy Birthday* as he blew out the candles, and he opened his present. The box turned into a waterfall of quarters.

As I woke up, her words from the dream were still vibrant. I had a message I needed to share; to help others feel love from beyond the clouds.

Happy birthday, Frank. Keep looking for the quarters. The love is there.

Saying goodbye to you was the hardest decision I ever had to make.

It broke my heart to know how sad
you'd be in the coming days.

It tore me apart,
knowing I couldn't comfort you.

As much as we talked, as much as I
shared and advised, it wasn't enough.

There's so much more I want you to know; so much more I want you to know about me, about life.

I wish I could have shielded you from all of life's struggles and disappointments... But they made you stronger.

I wish you could feel my heart bursting with joy, watching you grow into the person you are today.

I hope you know how proud
of you I was...

I was so proud and continue to smile at
your success.

I know it wasn't all perfect,
but please understand
I did the best I could at the moment
with the information
and resources I had.

As the hardest tears were cried and reality set in, I wanted to find a way to let you know my love is still here and that I'm not that far away.

Sometimes it seems magical.

I leave you quarters
when I think of a silly memory.

Grief is ripples of waves.
Sometimes it feels like a drizzle;
other times, it feels like
buckets of rain.

Just as you do, I feel the emptiness.

So, I leave you quarters where you'll find them.

I leave you quarters when your thoughts take you down memory lane.

Don't feel bad if there are moments
when you don't think of me.

I understand.

About the Author

Dr. Cheryl Robinson is an international speaker, founder of Creative Renegade Media & Ready2Roar and contributor for ForbesWomen with 27 Editors' Pick recognitions.

Having interviewed over 500 women and counting, she has had the fortunate opportunity to meet and engage with some of the most powerful, influential and inspiring women in the world, including Suzanne Shank, Kathleen Kennedy, Bobbi Brown, Diane von Furstenberg, Susie Wolff, Claire Williams, Christie Pearce Rampone, Maria Sharapova, La La Anthony, Melissa Rauch and Candace Cameron Bure.

As an international speaker, Cheryl has spoken, moderated and conducted workshops and panels for over 20 years. Her speaking portfolio includes engagements at Columbia University, Penn State, Columbia University/Oxbridge, Girl Meets World, Lakewood BlueClaws, the Acronis Women in Tech & Motorsports in Abu Dhabi and the U.N.'s Girl Up Teen Advisory Board.

Cheryl became a published author at the age of fourteen writing for the local newspaper. She's been published in multiple publications.

drcherylrobinson.com

www.ingramcontent.com/pod-product-compliance
Lightning Source LLC
Chambersburg PA
CBHW041308110426
42743CB00037B/33